THE REVENANT

POETRY
A Jump Start
After Ovid: New Metamorphoses
(co-edited with Michael Hofmann)

FICTION
The Silver Age
Three Evenings

THE REVENANT

James Lasdun

CAPE POETRY

First published 1995

1 3 5 7 9 10 8 6 4 2

© James Lasdun 1995

James Lasdun has asserted his right
under the Copyright, Designs and Patents Act, 1988
to be identified as the author of this work

First published in the United Kingdom in 1995 by
Jonathan Cape
Random House, 20 Vauxhall Bridge Road, London SW1V 2SA

Random House Australia (Pty) Limited
20 Alfred Street, Milsons Point, Sydney,
New South Wales 2061, Australia

Random House New Zealand Limited
18 Poland Road, Glenfield,
Auckland 10, New Zealand

Random House South Africa (Pty) Limited
PO Box 337, Bergvlei, South Africa

Random House UK Limited Reg. No. 954009

A CIP catalogue record for this book
is available from the British Library

ISBN 0-224-04144-4

Phototypeset by Intype, London
Printed in Great Britain by
Mackays of Chatham PLC

For Pia Davis

CONTENTS

ACKNOWLEDGEMENTS

Acknowledgements are due to the following: *Boulevard, London Review of Books, Paris Review, New Yorker, Pivot, After Ovid: New Metamorphoses, Poetry Review, Yale Review, Soho Square, Observer.*

'Zopilotes' was a prize-winner in the National Poetry Competition, 1993.

THE CALLING OF THE APOSTLE
MATTHEW

Not the abrupt way, frozen
In the one glance of a painter's frame,
Christ in the doorway pointing, Matthew's face
Bright with perplexity, the glaze
Of a lifetime at the counting house
Cracked in the split-second's bolt of being chosen,

But over the years, slowly,
Hinted at, an invisible curve;
Persistent bias always favouring
Backwardly the relinquished thing
Over the kept, the gold signet ring
Dropped in a beggar's bowl, the eye not fully

Comprehending the hand, not yet;
Heirloom damask thrust in a passing
Stranger's hand, the ceremonial saddle
(Looped coins, crushed clouds of inlaid pearl)
Given on an irresistible
Impulse to a servant. Where it sat,

A saddle-shaped emptiness
Briefly, obscurely brimming . . . Flagons,
Cellars of wine, then as impulse steadied
Into habit, habit to need,
Need to compulsion, the whole vineyard,
The land itself, groves, herds, the ancestral house,

Given away, each object's
Hollowed-out void successively
More vivid in him than the thing itself,
As if renouncing merely gave

Density to having; as if
He'd glimpsed in nothingness a derelict's

Secret of unabated,
Inverse possession . . . And only then,
Almost superfluous, does the figure
Step softly to the shelter door;
Casual, foreknown, almost familiar,
Calmly received, like someone long awaited.

WOMAN POLICE OFFICER IN ELEVATOR

Not that I'd ever noticed
Either a taste or a distaste
For that supposedly arousing
Rebus of pain and desire, the uniformed woman,
Whether as Dietrich in epaulettes,
Or armoured like Penthesileia, or in thigh-boots
And cocked hat, straddling the Atlantic,
Fishing for campesinos
With live torpedoes,

But when the rattling, john-sized
Tenement elevator paused
Mid-fall to blink a female housing cop
Into its humid cranium, I felt her presence
Spooling through me like a Möbius strip,
Splicing her spilling curls, nightstick, the gun at her hip,
Chrome shield, the breast it emblazoned,
Seamlessly into the same
Restless continuum . . .

I caught – was it possible? –
The scent of some sweet-tinctured oil;
Troubling, alluring; and looked away
Then glanced back obliquely: had I imagined it,
That sudden scimitar-glint of danger,
Or had some forbidden impulse – longing, lust, anger –
Tumid inside me like a hidden
Semi-automatic
In a schoolkid's lunchpack

Triggered the blue-lashed, tiny
Metal-detector of her eye?

3

I backed against my corner, watching
The numerals slowly swallow their green gulp of light;
Interminable! And as we fell,
Our little locked cube of stale air seemed to bristle
With a strange menace . . . I thought of harms;
My own and not my own,
Contemplated or done;

Betrayals, infidelities,
Coercions, seductions, lies,
Ready to confess them all, and more,
As if in her firm indifference she'd regressed me
Inward down some atavistic line
To the original essence, the masculine
Criminal salt; a frieze of victims
Panelled in my own skull
Like a lit cathedral hell . . .

A shudder, and then stillness;
Avoidance of each other's eyes
As in some bedroom fiasco's wake,
The air too brimful with disclosure, till the door
Opened and we parted, the clamped rift
Between us widening like a continental drift
Of the sexes; she to the butcher, the breaker,
The ripper, the rapist,
I to my therapist.

THE REVENANT

Jetlag, a jumpcut dawn, distempered
Daze of brickdust and rosedust,
Ache of memory, insomniac mumble of June;
The worst of absence is return,
Already not becoming what you once

Almost already were . . . Forgotten things
Forget themselves; the spellbound mirrors slumber
Dreaming of sand. A shut book dreams of lumber.
You wake them once a year,
Every year it gets harder.

Delicate hour,
Mica, translucent moon,
Hue of penitence (sham) on sleeping windows;
You walk to the borough gardens:
Locked, but a demolished house leads through,

And you stand in the exfoliated green of your own past,
Between the pond and the bench where the blind men sat;
Chestnuts ploughing the light – domed emerald rubble –
And a rain of birdsong gibbering like a language
You no longer speak or understand.

OXBLOOD

Mid–October, our Blackjack oak
Peppers the tar-paper roof with its ripened acorns;
Day and night, two weeks of it, Priapic
Scattershot clattering down
With every gust of wind from the mountain;
I stare outside. Impossible to sleep, think, work;

Into my mind a memory comes:
Another oak, the King Charles oak
That stood in our garden at home;
Survivor of summer lightning and winter storms,
The humps on its thick trunk bulging
Like muscles under the weight of its limbs.

One year half the buds withered
Before they'd opened. The rest stayed sickly yellow.
Oak-apples swelled on the twigs. Ringed ears of fungus
Sprouted from the scar of a lopped-off branch.
'Oxblood', the tree-doctor said,
And showed you where to dig it in.

The blood was granular, rich-smelling, moist, its crimson
Concentrated, masquerading as black:
I fingered it with a boy's
Professional interest in new substances:
Elixir of mud and fire; alchemic cack . . .
We dug it into the sloping lawn,

And waited – three years, four years,
Bad years, lithium years; lost jobs and breakdowns;
Your children's serial adolescence;
Once in a twilit hospital room

We watched your body sleeping on the bed;
Trespassers in the kingdom of the dead,

Bearing our modest gifts like ransom . . .
And then one spring the buds came strong again,
Lobed sprigs bubbling a haze, and like the stick
That blossomed when it stirred Medea's potion,
The tree burst into leaf again so thick
Its namesake could have hidden in its crown

All summer from his father's killers.
And I think of you now in your office, flourishing,
Bullish again, imperious, firing commands,
The silver claw-grip pencil firm in your hands,
Work warding off regret, age, doubt,
Catastrophe that stalks you through your friends,

Though if it should lay its regicidal axe
Against your neck, I think the cut would show
Not flesh but tree-rings circling back to zero,
And I wonder as I listen to this oak's
Triumphal drum, what sorceress filled your veins,
And who was the sacrificial ox.

CURATOR

i.m. John Caldwell

At six foot four you dwarfed your protégés
Whose pictures hung on the flaking paint
Of your East Village railroad apartment.
In your long absences the modest rooms,
Looking out on the hustlers of Saint Mark's Place
Through the indulgent eye of a dusty window,
Stood as your substitute, your understudy.
This was your home; its grain and shadow
Ran with your heart's own blood and breath:
It was almost you! Your antic melancholy;
Hot water ran from the cold tap in the bath . . .

This was your city too, if less
Lived in than longed for in other places;
The one soul-easing garden for a soul
Who disliked gardens, found the Great Outdoors
With its model's narcissistic smile
Downright suspect. This was all you needed
Of countryside: a subway's grove of girders
Lichened by graffiti, coiling
Creepers of razor wire, plus the odd
Hydrant bubbling like a forest spring . . .
Home! In our itinerant's sense of the word:

That which we do not live in. That which grows
Vaguer and more important every year.
Rumours of breakdown reached us from elsewhere;
Sickness, depression in San Francisco's
Too lushly green unshadowed atmosphere.
But here, here where we saw you last,

Cream-suited, a resplendent tan
Gilding your grin, you seemed yourself, your several
Dissonant selves resolved in one strong chord:
Anxious, avuncular, waspishly good-humoured,
Urbane East-Coaster, Tennessee Gentleman.

Last months: the fumbled endgame
Of one who seemed to side with circumstance
Against himself. You lost the flat,
Then cut loose cavalierly from the city,
Though even as you had your things shipped out,
You started plotting career moves back.
What had you seen too late? We watched the movers
Empty your sprawl of rooms into a truck;
Reckless, beloved friend! Scars blotched the walls
As if the things were torn from them by violence;
So in us your sudden absence hurts.

LIME PICKLE

Your father, not yet divorced,
Rosy-cheeked from the Garrick,
In his Savile Row pin-striped suit
Presided over the feast.

He spread the menu like a general's map,
Plotting his debauch
On the virginal palates
Of his teenage daughter and her first 'chap'.

In our singular innocence
We had tasted nothing stronger
Or stranger than each other's lips,
But your father's extravagance

(It broke him later)
Shoaling in salvers on the table
Under the tabla's gulp and throb,
And the moan of a sitar

Made our mouths water.
Unlidded, the dishes sizzled;
Sweet, spiced, sprinkled with edible gold;
A taste of our imminent future,

Though what I recall
Most clearly twenty years on
As I read his obit in *The Times*,
Is the spoonful of lime pickle

He tricked me into eating;
His harsh laughter
As it burned like a living coal
On my astounded tongue

Which however has learned
His own preference for mixed blessings,
Having grown sharper since then
And somewhat thicker-skinned.

OLIVE TREE

after Ovid

There already in the ploughlined
Face and brow, the knuckles'
Mud-blackened whorls, thin glinting eyes,
There in the goitred, squat, senescent frame,
Blunt lecherous hands made many in frantic groping,
There already the tree his flesh became —

Old Adam, Apulian Peasant
Who chased the nymphs through the garden
Till they turned on him and in their sudden
Unbluffed glances he felt an era ending
And withered into its epitaph —
Splayed feet anchoring

An old malevolence
Once and for all in history; sinews
Packed in woodgrain, inconsolable grief
Of a failing species
Croaking from his throat in bitter berries,
Every wink of his eye a little leaf.

LANDSCAPE WITH BUBBLES AND
BROOM

I watch the bubbles pearling on the ice
Of an early morning *spremuto*. As I drink,
The swaying ice cubes click and clink
And shower the fanlight of a lemonslice
With a fine silvery seethe of air.
My palate tingles. My head begins to clear . . .

Outside it's sunny. A sundial cypress
Vogues against the Tuscan stubble's
Cloth of gold. Hot air balloons like bubbles
Bulge from the earth . . . Inside, a TV hostess
Shimmies in lamé on a kitsch
Calcio theme-set . . . Apropos of which

You could have heard a pin drop
On the hotel lobby's salami-of-marble tile
When Baggio's ball sailed skyward and Brazil
Lobbed in the winner. Only the wry pop
Of a champagne cork reminded us defeat
Was somehow more . . . Italian. All night

Footballs bobbed in my dreams, and now I think
Of bubbles again. Bubbles! The very word
Almost unsayably absurd;
Its own brief globed and breaking blink,
Foaming a lightness through my own
Inclination to be stone . . .

Undust, unatom, matter's vowel,
Paradigm for the self-invented joke
Sidewinding out of its teller . . . Zero's cloak,
Mirror and ally of all things possible . . .

Now the balloons slide up. Their climb unlocks
The valleys *wunderkammer*, its treasure box –

Level on level of dovetailed slopes
Tumbling downward like the imprint
Of a vast pontifical pinecone; squint
Vineyards, olive groves, orchards; a hand-hewn landscape's
Novelistic casual-but-cunning detail;
Everything plotted, fitted into its petal-

Garden- or meadow-shaped slot of space
Just so,
And the sensational yellow
Broomflower banners wheeling down every crevice
As if the land were swiveling in gold light
Or popping with sprinkled dynamite

Or gilding itself for Guidoriccio's steed
To ride again . . . For surely a place must *want*
This added brilliance to let it run so rampant;
Christ! Even the birds are crested;
Little heralds, the local bugle call –
'All for glory, and enough glory for all'

Or possibly '*Forza Italia!*' given
How for the third time the lictor's rods
Have ousted the bucolic local gods –
Rings in your ear all day . . .
                              Now on the screen
The hostess *spanks* the ball for being bad.
It looks like something out of Kierkegaard;

Mankind 'astray in possibility',
Begging the question – that lamé swimsuit;
Is that what happens when a jackboot

Pupates: its billowing butterfly?
Is *sprezzatura* merely 'flatulent knowledge'?
No longer the fructifying pledge

Of the six red balls
Dancing on the Medici crest?
And lightness; the milky marble breast
Of Pisano's virgin, or Berlusconi's belles
So pumped you half expect the screens to rise
Like iridescent bubbles before your eyes?

Is there a difference? I drain my glass;
The used ice rustles: a fishlike, flat
Ghost of itself. The juice is also flat.
It needs its little spritz of nothingness
To give it life. Hence, doubtless, heaven
Likened in the gospels unto leaven.

'Hid in three measures of meal . . .'
Hence the sculptor's taste for marble's
Air- and light-loving calcite bubbles;
Hence the doctor's rod of sharpened steel
For plunging in your lung when it collapses,
Hence also the poet's weakness for ellipses . . .

I step outside. The broomflower's soapy smell
Drifts on the breeze . . . Hard not to feel a strange
Volatile happiness here, as if a change
Of shape were always imminent; that sparkle
Of salt-light on the sky's crushed lapis dome
Venus perpetually rising from the foam . . .

POWDER COMPACT

Twenties, machine-age cloisonné, steel lines
Shimmying through the enamel plaque,
Priced voluptuously – as I wrote the cheque
My new love surged on its own extravagance –
Nocturnal, businesslike, here was your brisk
Sinuous walk, your pagan/puritan air –
It was like buying you in miniature . . .
I didn't look inside. A stifling musk
Burst on us as you opened it: the past;
The original owner's scented powder puff –
That's all. I didn't catch *memento mori*
Whispered in her spilt, too intimate dust
Till now, or read in hers, love's epitaph
Still pink and scut-soft in its reliquary.

TIMING

The secret of good comedy. Ours was bad,
A hot-house passion blooming under force
Of imminent separation. Were our eyes
Bigger than our hearts? A candlebud
Of amaryllis burned for you in my room
Three thousand miles away. You stalled your visit
Twice, mysteriously, and came too late.
Our out-of-sync phonecalls were a bad dream –
Echolocation of love! My lopped bromeliad's
Adze-stumps turned to black bronze as you rode
The planet into light, five hours ahead.
Even when you came we lived in shifts,
Watching the amaryllis' oxblood explode;
Ten days of brilliance, then abruptly dead.

GENERAL McCLELLAN

Pride, questioner, and pride's obverse, fear;
Fear of failure. *The Times* of London
Noted my Air of Success. Our grand
Potomac army loved me as I'd planned.
I was Napoleon. I snubbed Lincoln.
Think if I'd obeyed him: one swift strike,
Rebellion over, slavery intact
Oneself in office . . . I couldn't act.
What if I should fail? My ranks
Glistened like the river in its banks;
Beautiful, swollen to bursting . . . I held them back,
Fattening like a calf for Lee's attack
Now freedom that couldn't use me as a spear
Rises on my inertia like a jack.

BAROQUE

(Borromini: 1599–1667)

Spirit and form; to every soul its shell;
Sounds their instruments – flute, double bass,
Trumpet, each instrument its plush-lined case,
The flesh its cribs, Death its Heaven and Hell.
Bernini, your lightest-fingered rival,
Built only on the human scale, filled Rome
With wooing, delicious airs; *your* dome,
Dizzying, serial-spiralled, was a skull
Sucked to the coffered contours of a mind
Breached by infinity. The Infinite!
It made you less as well as more than human;
Implosive, visionary, one hand designed,
The other flogged a workman till he died,
Then drew the sword you fell on like a Roman.

Back, and as if a spell
Had broken, I could almost
Bring myself to open what I'd closed
For seven years; your image, vector
Of disappointments, and speak in the tone of the shriven.
So in that deep street's swiftly decanting dazzle
I fell in step with our seven years' younger selves
And like an objective ghost

Saw us for what we were,
Which was to say more or less
As others, each other's best but wrong guess.
This was our quarter: butcher, fabbro
This was our doorway; impregnable, seven years thick,
Behind it our dark flat with its summer furniture,
Brick alcove I stood in forming words you watched me
Almost utter then suppress.

Others are in there now,
It gives itself to their lives,
Offers them in its eaves and alcoves
Substance tractable to memory;
Says: 'for this contentment, boredom, sadness,
Here is an afternoon silence, out there a fabbro,
His can of smoking varnish, his bulls-horn anvil,
There the lanceolate leaves

Of an oleander;
Assume this contingency
Into your days here as the tree
Drinks from beneath these salmon-scale cobbles
Its globe of shivering leaves . . .' Bells rang, the day was
    passing

Crying in tongues: *one life only to transfigure,*
And as if I'd switched sides in a train
And what once rushed to meet me

Started slipping away,
I felt wrenched forward, estranged,
While everything – street, sky, you – seemed plunged
In valedictory shadow; old photographs
Of faces in which a posthumous knowledge
Had worked a premonitory sorrow in each eye,
An almost visible change of expression . . .
Otherwise nothing had changed.

SONG

Anhedonic,
Spooling like a depression,
Blinder with every block to the littered green,
The High Street stitches a psychic
Winter out of your footsteps'
Proserpinal return.

Ailing too long
The body at last desists
From craving or even wanting back its once
Healthy complexion and pink tongue
Who needs to die twice over?
Leave us our stricken streets.

' – Am black because
The sun hath looked upon me – '
Where was that, brother? Not in this town surely;
Here where the damp blooms swastikas
And a beer-can held to the ear
Whispers fuck off and die;

Where the banked crates
Outside the Carib grocer
Hold their shrivelled chillies and fibrous ginger,
Frost-rotted peppers and starfruits
Like a disintegrating
Memory of fire,

And the fume-browned
Lantern cover of heaven
Hides neither a friendly nor a vicious grin,
Transstellar paradise, pearl-veined,
Nor Southern Cross: just circling
Planes, a salt beach of moon.

BAG-SLASHERS IN THE TERMINAL TERRESTRE

Pack slung from each shoulder, wads
Of soft cash in every pocket,
Locked on instantly by three pairs of eyes,
Caged victim fattened for sacrifice
To the latter-day war-gods or hell-gods,
He fumbles in his shirt to buy a ticket –

They move in: two men, a boy –
Goblins out of an alkali nightmare
Or out of the pages of Bernal Diaz; a pair
Of *Papas* and their catamite (hair clotted
With blood from the twelve or more captives a day
Unpacked, dismembered, eaten, the temple walls spattered

Black till the Spaniards brought whitewash,
Lime, clean altar-cloths and roses
As if they could fumigate the human
Psyche itself, or teach obsidian
It wasn't right to open human flesh –)
Dimly their target stirs, but the sprung trap closes;

Atavistic gesture
Scissoring out of shadow, felt
Not as sensation but a pang of knowledge
Opening in an abrupt coiled
Braid of shuddering buses, soot-belch,
Incense, blade-flash, terror,

And there in the bright force-field
Of his own shock, he thumbs apart
The slashed-through canvas of his bag – and from his face

You'd think them agents of an unsuspected grace
Lighting him like a candle as they melt
Back through the years to the crash of his woken heart.

ZOPILOTES

Between two villages where the rows
Of agave thin to a scrub of crabgrass
And red clay slung like a gaunt pelt
Over a pelvis of rocks; beside a road
Melting out into oiled air either end
The body of a horse lies where it fell,
In a rigging of entrails; plundered skull
Bleaching to socketed chalk. A vulture
Caged like a great black heart in its tattered hull
Eases her neck out between two ribs,
Twists, and croaks skyward where her mate
Wheels in the blue. Before he drops
She steps from the belly, preens her ruff, and chooses,
Assiduously, a gobbet of flesh, then hops
Onto the wobbling carcass, and as he lands
Jabs it into his mouth. And there,
On a bed of carrion with clattering bones for springs,
In a studious rapture, as if intent
On probing the outer dustward limits of flesh,
They couple — two scorched angels; connoisseurs
Of fallenness; apostate saints of love;
Fanning a black-flamed blaze with their beating wings.

AZTEC HOTEL

for Michael Hofmann

Staying on; the imagined future of a coast
Opened like Tenochtitlan to the white men,
Who never came: a bauhaus/barracks ruin,
Terrace and private bath for every ghost.
The sun drifts like a coin in oil. A swarm
Of winged priests, each its own obsidian knife,
Murders the feathered serpent into life;
Their bodies swell and redden on my arm . . .
Verdigris'd whitewash, crimson bougainvillaea
Spurting from concrete pillars like a wrist's
First leap of blood . . . A set of six chrome rungs
Drops to a hot blue void; despair –
A dry pool where a bald hen roosts,
Quetzalcoatl cackling on stone tongues.

NARCISSUS

Sometimes I almost have you then I don't:
Always one frame ahead of me you move
Into a room, talk, close your eyes, make love;
I copy every gesture but I can't
Quite catch you up. As accidental others
Reeled into family photographs, your soul
Must have been turned round idly like a jewel
In the mind's eyes of strangers; schoolfriends' mothers,
Shopkeepers, waitresses — what did they see?
How did they misconceive you? Or did one
Happen to catch the stone's full fissured dazzle?
I know you less than even so glancingly;
I, who should be closer to you than son
Or lover. I'm not even on your trail.

US & THEM

They said some encouraging things
What more could they have said?
Assuming a difference between
The look that judges and the look that loves,
Happier versions of ourselves go by

For instance down a corridor,
And when a new face turns from a room,
Stand still as if the lino floor
Had grown a golden-headed flower,
Loving the world that gave them this.

PLAGUE YEARS

There is, it would seem, in the dimensional scale of the world, a kind of delicate meeting place between imagination and knowledge, a point, arrived at by diminishing large things and enlarging small ones, that is intrinsically artistic.

(Nabokov, *Speak, Memory*)

Sore throat, persistent cough . . . The campus doctor
Tells me 'just to be safe' to take the test.
The clinic protocol seems to insist
On an ironic calm. I hold my fear.
He draws a vial of blood for the City Lab,
I have to take it there, but first I teach
A class on Nabokov. Midway I reach
Into my bag for *Speak, Memory*, and grab
The hot bright vial instead. I seem at once
Wrenched from the quizzical faces of my class
Into some silent ante-room of hell:
The 'delicate meeting place'; I feel it pounce;
Terror – my life impacted in the glass
My death enormous in its scarlet grail.

THE RECOVERY

Goodbye Bronxville gothic
So long forever Fleetwood tudor;
I'll miss my borrowed office
Where I traced a persistent smell of bitter ashes
To a pot-pourri of moth wings
Scorching in the globe lamp.

I'll miss the oily, ice-gravelled river
With its junk of half-swallowed car-wrecks
Glinting down through the suburbs of Wakefield and
    Woodlawn,
And the podiatrist's ad on its rain-puckered billboard:
One-Eight-Hundred WHY HURT?
One-Eight-Hundred END PAIN.

It was Sexual Harassment Awareness Week
When the egg-sized magnolia buds.
Crashed all over campus.
In little jets and bunches the green
Apparently still resilient Beyond
Broke from the tip of each twig like silk from a wand

Or the eyes of a former lover
Waking somewhat bemused to find you there;
You, who thought you could no more turn over
A new leaf, than the river
Heal its old hulls and disgorge them
Pristine, abluted, ticking like polished watches . . .

FIRST BODIES

All evening the herds stream from the woods
Down the Interstate, the Palisades,
Dreamy-eyed, tiptoeing does and coral-crowned bucks
Crossing over the water to Manhattan,
Strapped onto roof-racks and the backs of pick-up
    trucks,
Scooped muzzles open as if to nibble
Ribbons of bark, sprigs of bittersweet.

Still more themselves than anything else
(Scut-hearts flush as milkweed under tails),
They flare through the city in a soft, slow-motion
Fusillade; as estranging, as out of place
Among the iron and cobbles, the calypygean
Bubble-strut of graffiti, as the lead
Lodged in their tight flesh, or as the men,

The blue- or white-collared blood-brothers
Who got up early in the boroughs
To take their thirsty souls into the wilderness
And drink to the dregs its elixir of bright
Silence and ungridded space, from the tipped black
    glass
Of cross-hair sights angled through flensed white birch,
Maple scrub and crimson-burred sumac

With a sudden sweet kick of betrayal,
Half-wished, half not what was meant at all,
Gun-smoke and dropped knees insufficient to express
The vanishing tumult of consummation
Or that in spite of appearances tenderness
Was probably the point: love as violence;
Its usual name in the fallen world.

THE ACCOMPLICES

A small man thumbed us down and sidled in
Dusting the seat with a quick flick first, his wrist
Thin enough to snap like a candy bar;
Runt-of-the-litter frame, mid-twenties, shivering,
A little drunk, 'You folks
Headed for Cromar's Hatch?' We weren't
But the day being cold, and this good turn so easy,
We said we'd take him just the same.
He thanked us, then with a sly glance at the mirror,
Added 'I just got out
From the St Johnsbury Penitentiary
I was in for some shit I did.'

The road he led us on fell steeply twisting
Down so far from the winter altitudes
We hit Vermont's fifth season two weeks early;
Mud season, poverty's own;
Our four wheels thrashed in a cold lava
As we inched a dream-slow progress
Into an unenchanted land
Of trailers on rotting blocks, junked sno-mobiles,
Cracked satellite dishes, the five-car households,
Each car deeper in slurry than the last,
Till we came to a low-slung house with a line of smoke
Wobbling on its chimney, and a yard
Matted with flattened stalks
Fleshy and yellow from the winter.

'You can stop here mister.'
Our passenger climbed out,
Thanked us again, then leaned back down to the car
And whispered with a confidential grin

'Reckon my woman's in for a shock, kid too,
I ain't supposed to visit since what I did.'

There was a moment while he let himself in;
A puzzled hush; the body's
Quicker apprehension than the mind's
Of something not right – till the meaning of his words
Welled up into their sounds and crystalled out
Stealing across us like a film of ice
Urging my arm to the wheel to heave it round
And move us out of there before we saw,
Before we could see the literal
Matter of his words, his *what I did*,
As if a willed blindness could dispose
Of any lesson in complicity;
The inextricable bad in good intentions
That shadows them from the start – the counterpoise
That levers them up into light;
As if we didn't fear our own darknesses enough
To have dreamed already the child
Who stepped out from the doorway
As our tyres whirled, moving us too slowly
Not to watch its approach,
Apple-cheeked first, but up closer
More pumpkin than apple;
Gashed and swollen like an old pumpkin,
A jack-o'-lantern without the candle-flicker,
Welted legs rickety as bamboo,
Tottering towards us as if to ascertain
What manner of creature held sway
Over its father's coming and goings,
While from our held breath we might have been
     watching
An opossum or another of those shy animals
Rumoured to be in abundance but seldom seen.

INTERSTATE

Lights, inaction . . . Of what
Force is this the imbricate form,
This mailed sinew of traffic slowed to a snake-crawl
Where the state capital rears its gorgon-shocked
Tentacular mesh of bridges and intersections
Over the birch-brake and rainbow-smeared marshes
In the blackening crystal of November?

Ahead sputtering flares
Cordon the accident; oils spew
Out of a buckled Buick stupidly askew:
Simplified expressiveness of machinery;
Formal panic of patrol car lights; concern
Of probing helicopters; stylized welcome
(Palms outward like a stone god's at a tomb)

Of the ambulance's
Rear doors open for the body
Bundled in its blooded swaddling on the asphalt.
Blood swings toward blood; the branch of veins lurching
Like a dowsing rod in the gut . . . Now four tall buildings,
Reading each other's paragraphs of light
Coil us into their chambers;

Each mind sensing remote
Loss as of distant cliffs crumbling.

THE PLAGUE AT AEGINA

after Ovid

Cephalus at Aegina, not a face
Familiar on the skiffs or landing place;
With a discreet glance round he notes their features:
Hard, thin-lipped, pallid, 'Aeacus these creatures
Milling in silence on the quays seem . . . odd,
Not quite, if you'll permit me, flesh and blood;
Pin-pupilled as if flushed from underground,
And this eerie silence! Not a human sound;
No cheer, no cry of greeting, not a voice
Raised for my ships . . . Where are they now, the boys
Who ran with me before through the game-crammed
    woods
With slings and javelins, young men built like gods,
And the women Aeacus, with sparkling eyes
Who kept me company at the sacrifice,
Soft laughter on their lips as they threw the garlands
Into the embers forging our alliance,
Where are they now? And the clowns, the leopard
    tamers,
Dancers and jugglers who matched me at our famous
Revels drink for drink till the sun came up
Firing the sands like wine spilt from a cup?'
To which Aeacus with the abrupt frown
Of one whom the memory of loss casts down
As bleakly as the loss itself, replied
'In their graves Cephalus; our kingdom's pride
Trampled like ripening cornstalks by some vague
Vaporous army . . . Cephalus a plague
Was granted us by the gods; a pestilence
That made an equal mockery of science

And prayer. No hope was left us but the hope
Of a quick death . . . Look, where the forests slope
Down from the mountains; there – some say from the
    spite
Of Jove's spurned jealous goddess at the sight
Merely of shadow-seeking human love
Minding its business in a quiet grove
The disease began. From there it spread to town
Where like an artist coming into his own
It turned prolific, spewing its singular species
Of sculpture by the cartload; masterpieces
Of corpsework, moulding its sumptuous cadavers
Out of prime flesh – young warriors, athletes, lovers;
First it blew on their innards like a coal
Till their skin flushed and sweat began to roll
Profusely from every pore, then swelled their tongues
And set a racking spasm in their lungs
So that each difficult breath came like the knife
Of a skilled torturer prolonging life
Only to lengthen pain. Meanwhile its brush
Stippled black sores across the wasting flesh
Till even the softest linen seemed to scour,
And victims writhed face downward on the floor
As if intent on hastening their own
Reunion with the nerveless realm of stone.
Then, Cephalus, their suffering began;
A kind of teeming numbness overran
Their senses: hearing, taste, smell, touch, then sight,
Eclipsing till unmitigated night
Gripped them, and then came madness, the mind's own
Catabolic horrors, mushroom-grown
In the putrescence of itself . . . Great dismal
Moth wings flapping in the skull, phantasmal
Demons with scourges . . .' Here the king broke off,
Staring a moment at his guest. 'Enough.

Suffice it that death was welcome when it came
Though the disease still sputtered like a flame
In the dead corpse, and just as before their ends
The sick infected doctors, family, friends,
So the dead also laboured in the slaughter,
Seeping the sickness out into earth and water,
Coiling it into the air like rotting meat
As their piled-up bodies mounted in the street
Too fast for us to bury them . . . Each breath
Seemed a deliberate overture to death;
Every drop of water or crumb of bread
Weighed on the tongue like coins the already dead
Bring for the ferryman; a living hand
Brushed in passing seared one like a brand
With terror of death . . . How could we not despair,
Those of us still living, when the mere
Fact of being human was like a crime
Punishable by torture at the whim
Of a capricious tyrant? Some attempted
To outmanoeuvre fate by suicide:
Afflicted logic. Others gave away
All they possessed and left their homes to pray
For mercy in the temples, where they died:
Congregations of corpses side by side,
As ineffectual then in dumb reproach
As in loud pious prayer before. Soon each
Citizen withdrew into a dull
Apathy, or best a cynical
Contempt for life, for all that promised once
Superabundant pleasure to every sense,
For what in their own flesh once used to surge
Obediently at life's replicating urge –
Mantis rapture in which our bodies swim
A moment till it rips us limb from limb . . .
So our survivors crept through the mausoleum

Our once convivial island had become;
Frightened, shunning each other as they drifted
Past silent buildings, ghostlier than the dead;
Too few of us, and those too young or old
To till the neglected fields, hunt deer, rebuild
Houses on unpolluted land, clean wells,
Or grind our scavenged corn at the rusting mills,
So that those plague had spared now seemed condemned
To die of cold or hunger, the whole race doomed!
For what? What sin, what crime against the gods
Could merit that?
                    One evening in the woods
(The same you spoke of Cephalus, where you hunted
With the young men I gave you, all since dead),
While searching for birds' eggs like the humblest
Of my own subjects, reaching for a nest
In an old oak, I saw a moving column
Of ants returning up a twisting limb
Into the hollow trunk. Some carried grains
Twice their own size, some linked in living chains
Round battling moths or beetles that others dragged
Homeward like enemy hostages. None lagged
Or idled on the march – if empty-jawed
They formed impromptu regiments and warred
On other stray rivals, or helped a neighbour;
Thousands of them, teeming in silent labour
Along the furrowed ridges . . . I who'd lost
As many people, watched this swarming host
In a strange dreamlike anguish . . . Falling down
Onto my knees, I cried out 'Father of Heaven,
Maker of earth and sky and all that lives,
You whom this fanatic order gives
Less offence, it seems, than our own human
Muddle of blind desire and fumbling vision,
Grant me people like these, since you favour them,

And in such numbers; fill my empty kingdom
With a new race of men.'
                              At once the tree's
Branches started to shake, though not a breeze
Disturbed the air. I felt my own limbs tremble,
My hair rise as the ants began to tumble
Onto the ground beside me where they raised
Their armoured bodies up. I watched amazed
As inch by inch they grew before my eyes:
Hind legs stretching and swelling to human size,
Heads bulging, torsos bloating out to burnished
Breastplates, mid-limbs shrinking till they vanished,
And in the shape of men they filled the woods
Silently in massed ranks spreading backwards
Far as the eye could see. Then each one raising
A new-formed arm, they hailed me as their king.

These are the men and women Cephalus
You see before you now; my insect race,
Just as I'd asked for in my prayer to Jove.
As you might guess from my description, Love,
That once amused us with its faithful cast
Of fluttering Crushes, over-perfumed Lust,
Passion's soprano foghorn wailing in vain
At Vanity, Suspicion with his pain,
Hasn't found great favour with these creatures,
And though this touch of coldness in their natures
Is more than balanced by their loyalty,
No king was ever more estranged than I
From his own populace. But let that pass,
They're thrifty, disciplined, industrious,
Brutal in battle. I call them Myrmidons
In memory of their milling origins.
They'll follow you obediently in the wars
Our treaty binds us in. Take them, they're yours.'

EDEN

Winter, nighttime, Jane Street and West Fourth,
Three blocks east of the Hudson, brownstones
    trussed
In garters of lacy black wrought iron,
Steam-spooks and gravelled moonlight, frost . . .

It might have been the second night of creation;
Stellar silence, a triple-locked
Empty universe waiting for the first spoor
To lug its baggage five flights to the door –

For two days I didn't unpack.
I liked the ringing air distilled
Out of bare walls and empty shelves,
The whiff of promise not yet unfulfilled,

I could be anyone; I bought three vast
Elaborate tropical stems – a token
Of the man I was to become:
Freed, flamboyant, bigger-hearted . . .

I watched a tongue unfurl, fanned ganglia,
Dewlaps, a clutch of hatching parakeets
The room swarmed in a puce light –
I couldn't wait for them to die;

It seemed they never would: the coil and bloom
Convulsive, intimate; a masque of carnage –
Adam, Eve and Lilith, one stem each,
As if they'd sprouted from my own flesh.

In June the prehistoric gingkos
Swam veinless leaves through the greased, sizzling air,

We lay in the emerald swamplight
Listening to the monkey yelp of sirens –

Dawn was the dawn of time: Triceratops
Hauled its meat off the screen at Naturemax
And rumbled down Columbus.
I woke to hear it snuffling in the garbage.

LINES FOR A CIVIC STATUE

The president takes a ceremonial stroll
Among the sequoias. His mandate is euphoria;
The coin-calm lake at the end of history,
Golf lessons in the forsythia suburbs,
Xmas in the Poconos where Moses
Shall con the waters of their livid rainbow.

Tomorrow stands in a doorway watching his maker's
Body probe itself for a vein;
Narrowed intelligence of inchworm groping for
    footing –
Now is a place he's in but won't be soon;
He has inherited his estate in winter;
When the snow melts he'll find what fresh wonders await
    him.

Midnight evacuates the day –
A mighty city emptied of its people
A mighty people cheated of its city
Under the embers a brand new adorable creature
Forges its feathers, builds its own beak of bronze,
Wrecking-yard talons strong to crush coachfuls of
    children.

Upturned, the ship of freedom was an axe;
Men to much misery and hardship born
Learning mayhem as a child learns how to read,
In tentative steps, toiling at study –
'What are eyes for?' 'Eyes are for blinding.'
'Why do fingers crook?' 'For the crooked trigger.'

MONDAY MORNING, PENN STATION

Stalled in the NJ Transit room
I watch the derelict inmates bum
Quarters for coffee. Violent white
Blizzards from neon day and night,
Not light but the dead ash of light
Fluorescing stubble, sores, the stung
Familiar flesh; I turn, my tongue
Sours in its yellow caffeine swill.
Out on the street a vendor's stall
Sells rubble from the Berlin Wall
In little chamois bags: rejoice;
Sing free enterprise, free choice,

Freedom! The windows of my train
Show a glassy smoke like crinoline
Crinkling the light on factory stacks;
Almost gorgeous sarcoma slags
Of black waste glitter like a dream's
Distant indefinite horror; streams
Trap in ice electric swirls
Of pink, blue, and mint-green overspills;
Stropped liquid razors to the salmon gills
(Never to break loose like Lowell's);
Swollen planet, bloated ball,
Is it for this the mighty fall?

That the one inalienable right
Be the pursuit of appetite;
That a new race of men arise
With a new hunger in their eyes;
Knowing neither pain nor terror,
Whose only altar is a mirror;
Hurling across the woods and plains

43

A million bilious fast-food chains,
Till the next toppled tyrant's wife,
Running in circles for her life
Clucks like a hen 'Alack, Alack',
And drops with a bullet in her back?

In labyrinths and forests stand
Imagined hybrids, hoofed and horned,
Sniffing the slumped, malignant air
For the scent of something new and pure;
Virgin, unblemished by the touch
Of their own words or of their flesh –
Myths for the mired: to be cleansed each year;
The undiscredited idea
Flushing the mind like lust, till it
Dims, then the next, then the next, then what?
Mankind tormented unicorn
Where will you dip your poisoned horn?

ERYSICHTHON

after Ovid

for Nicholas Jenkins

I

The scene: a town under mountains;
Clapboard, shingle and brick, the usual
Straggle of shopping malls, post-colonial
Factory outlets and fast-food chains
Thinning upward through scant
Cattle pastures then woods
Where the hulk of a disused chemical plant

Drips and leaks. This was built by one
Erysichthon, who as it happens
Also built the malls and the fast-food chains,
Outlets too – in fact who'd built the town,
Downtown at least, who owned
A piece of everything;
And several pieces of the board who'd zoned

Or rather rezoned certain lands
Once listed 'Grade A Conservation'
As 'Grade E, Suitable for Speculation',
Placing in their benefactor's hands
The local beauty spots
Which he, magician-like,
Tore to pieces and turned into parking lots,

Malls, outlets, chains, etcetera.
This is our hero, Erysichthon;
Ex-boxer, self-styled entrepreneur, ex-con

(Wire fraud, two years in a white-collar
'Country Club') after which
The town received him back
With open arms. Why not? He'd made them rich,

Some of them anyway, besides
He had a certain big man's swagger
People admire; a cross between an ogre
And Father Christmas: three hundred pounds,
Bearded, built like a vat,
With a great booming voice
And a cuff on the chin that could knock you flat.

He and his daughter, a shy girl
Who doted on him in a perverse
Return for his neglect, abuse or worse,
Lived in a ramshackle gothic pile
With its own pool and grounds
Planned by himself, put up
By his own men, and just as he cheated friends,

So he'd managed to cheat himself:
Cheap timbers warping, shoddy brickwork
Damp on the plastered insides, outside a murk
Of crooked-lined mortar; not a shelf,
Door or cupboard nailed straight,
The skimped-on pipes bursting
Every winter . . . Yet over this second-rate

Botched-up construction seemed to float
A yearning, an almost palpable
Dream of grandeur and splendour, of epic scale –
Vintage cars on the drive, a power boat
Dry-docked in the garage,
Barbecues big enough
For hogs and oxes on the tilting acreage

Of the rear porch: pure appetite
So strong at first glance it seemed to change
Will into deed, so that briefly by a strange
Hypnotism you transformed the sight
Into its own ideal,
Pinnaced and shimmering,
As if he'd tripped you up on some hidden zeal

You yourself harboured for excess . . .
This was his secret; to sell his clients
On their own luck-rich dreams. The plant for instance
(Electrolyte for capacitors) –
He'd lured the company
Less by the usual talk
Of tax breaks, kickbacks, etcetera, than by

Some potent, invisible
Spume of unlimited confidence
That reached them from his squat bulk like the hormones
By which certain animals compel
Others to roll over
And get shafted, which was
Precisely what they did. Within a year

The concrete floor had fissured. Waste
Seeped through the cracks. Teratogenic
(Lit: 'monster-breeding') PCBs and toxic
Potions to suit every other taste
Were found in a nearby
Spring-fed pool where hunters
Told of seeing at twilight an unearthly

Fluorescence in the reeds, of strange
Deformities in local creatures:

Web-footed mice, snakes with fur in patches,
Dropped antlers with a bluish mineral tinge . . .
True or not, the place shut
And for a while our man
Was banned from the trade. But genius will out,

And in his retreat from the world
(This was how he preferred to term it)
He had a vision, as befits a hermit:
Before him a spread of trees unfurled –
A radiant, flower-filled wood
With a clearing in which
Clusters of brand new sunshot houses stood.

Luxury homes; but more than just
Luxurious (and this is what we mean
By genius); he'd design the whole thing green!
What? Erysichthon turned ecologist?
Apparently. No scam
Surely could bring such pious
Tears to his eyes; 'I'm green, I really am,'

He said out loud as a swell
Of righteousness filled his heart: 'I'll build
Windmills and solar panels, use recycled
Paper for prospectuses, and sell
Not houses but ideals
Carved in organic forms
From eco-friendly natural materials . . .

Let's say a million bucks apiece
Which isn't much considering
How good you'll feel just living there and saving
The earth, in fact it's cheap at the price.'
So to the zoning board

Whose members could be seen
Later that year at choice resorts abroad

Sunning themselves, expenses paid.
Then to the S & L, a boardroom lunch
To pitch for funds: 'My friends I have a hunch
That one day on our children's lips Cascade – '
(His name for the project)
'Will be a word for hope;
A word for how we didn't self-destruct,

A word for courage, for the best
In our great nation under God, the true
Spirit of enterprise, get-up-and-go, can-do;
Call me a bleeding heart, an idealist,
Call me a renegade
Liberal, but my friends
I have a hunch that history wants Cascade –

I have a hunch that one day we
Who built it will have built a paradise
Sung with our fruited plains and spacious skies
Praised with our purple mountains' majesty . . .'
And so on till the air
Filled with directors' sobs.
'We're in,' they cried, 'we're green, we really are.'

II

High above town a first-growth wood
Fanned out from a crease in the mountain
Where waterfalls churned a mist like pile-driven
Marble dust; a sparkling quarry cloud
On which a rainbow played.
This was the lucky site
Our hero had selected for Cascade,

Though to a certain sect in town,
Keepers of a certain mystic flame,
The wood had long been known by another name:
The White and Blue. In spring the waving crown
Of dogwood and hawthorn trees
Formed a white cumulus
Of blossom above, while like a tapestry's

Millefleur background, an undergrowth
Of cream-coloured wildflowers spread below –
Featherbells, sweet white violets, moonseed, yarrow,
Trembling wood-anemones – till the earth
Foamed like a breaking wave
With living surf. And then,
As spring passed, blue, the blue of a chapel nave

Under a blue rose window rose
Like a blue-blooded blush into the white;
Wild hyacinth, hyssop skullcap, aconite,
Blooming over the ground while buckthorn sloes
And juniper berries
Hung ripening above.
Here our sect, a sisterhood of Ceres –

White witches mostly – assorted
Healers, herbalists and hierophants
Of Wicca – came each month to gather plants:
Cohosh, lobelia roots, enchanter's nightshade,
White milkweed for the heart,
Emetic gentian; raw
Matter for every magic or mystic art.

Needless to say the White and Blue
Was precious to them, and when the word
Of Cascade reached their ears, they flew to the wood,

Arriving just as Erysichthon's crew
Were unloading chainsaws.
Circling a central stand
Of ancient trees they cried 'This wood is ours,

Sacred to our goddess: touch it
And our curse be on your heads.' The crew
Hung back: in this uncertain era few
Had quite the rashness not to admit
At least a vague belief
In most things spiritual –
Curses, auras, Atlantis, an afterlife

On other planets; however,
Our hero, drunk on his rhetoric
Had lathered up an almost messianic
Zeal for his project, and a quiver
Of indignation shook
His great bulk as he learned
Of this pious protest. Jumping in his truck

And barrelling up to the wood,
Where he found the women hand in hand
Stalling his men, he bellowed 'This is my land,
Let me get at those trees or you're as good
As lumber yourselves. I paid – '
(Grabbing a chainsaw here)
' – My money now I've come to build Cascade.'

And, holding out the saw, he strode
Towards the protestors. One of them,
A grey-haired, soft-spoken woman by the name
Of Gendenwitha (Iroquois word
For Day Star), gently stepped
Out of the ring and spoke
Of her own ancestors who'd worshipped

In this very spot; of how each
Tree was once thought to contain a soul
'So that to chop – ' but with a contemptuous snarl
Erysichthon cut her off mid-speech,
Giving the starter cord
Of his chainsaw a yank,
And revving the engine till the big blade roared

Violently into life; and so,
Wielding it wildly in front of him,
He cut through an iron-hard hornbeam, lopped each
     limb
Of an oak from its trunk, and as though
The mutilated stump
Woke some demon in him,
He rampaged through the wood; slashed out at a clump

Of hazels that leapt like soldiers
Blown from a trench . . . Pines and birches fell
Under the swipe of his blade, a sour smell
Of sap rose into the air, loud cries
From the scattered women
Running from tree to tree
Vied with the chainsaw roar, and seemed to madden

Their enemy into a state
Of apoplectic outrage . . . Up ahead
He saw a great blossoming tree, a dogwood
Held by some to house the wood's own spirit;
Gashing it with his blade
He sprang back in surprise:
Out of the wound poured sap the colour of blood:

A scarlet banner unfurling
Into the *White and Blue* . . . and then the tall

Glittering dome of the tree began to fall;
Twisting, the leaves and blossom swirling,
Trunk splintering like a bone,
And as it crashed, the whole
Wood and hillside echoed with the groan.

III

Meanwhile Gendenwitha came
To the waterfall, where on her knees
She prayed out loud: 'Demeter, Ishtar, Ceres,
Papothkwe (to use my people's name) –
Life force of every plant;
You whose reality
We've honoured to this day in blind faith, grant

Some token of yourself, and if
Our love can't bring you into being
Then let this man's brutality.' So saying,
She looked up at the foam-curtained cliff
And in the rainbow glaze
Saw suddenly the bright
Voluptuous shimmering figure of the goddess.

Trembling, dazzled, she heard a voice
Close in her ear like a rush of wind
Whisper 'Daughter, follow this stream till you find
A cinderblock shack. This is the House
Of Hunger. Go inside,
Tell Hunger to visit
Erysichthon.' With which the vision faded.

So the woman set out along
The twisting stream that led through the wood
Where its pure waters took on a tint of blood

From the sacred tree. From there the long
Fall past fields and quarries,
Cities, suburbs, thruways,
Stockyards and junkyards, strip-mines, foundries,
    factories

Added a number of other
Interesting tints to the stream – spilt oil,
Solvents, pesticides, slurries, lead – until
Nothing was left for Gendenwitha
To follow but a thin
Ooze of mud-coloured sludge
That crawled across a desolate moonlike plain

Of exhausted farmland; barren,
Skeletal orchards, rusting silos,
Dry irrigation pipes crisscrossing meadows
Of dust, with here and there a warren
Of crooked-chimneyed huts,
Slumped trailers where old cars
Sank in the mud out front, and starving mutts

Skulked by trashcans; till at last
A little cinderblock shack appeared:
Doorless, derelict-looking . . . The woman peered
Into the shadows. There in the dust
Sat a hollow-eyed child
Dressed in rags, neglected;
Over her wizened, listless face hung soiled

Clumps of thin hair; her lips were cracked,
Sores crusted her throat, her brittle bones
Stuck out under her scooped-out shoulders and loins,
And long claws seemed to have gouged the racked
Furrows in her ribcage.

This was Hunger. A spoon
Dangled from her hand, and a look of reproach,

Ancient and unappeasable,
Glistened in her eyes. Without a word
She listened to Ceres' commands and followed
The woman back up the stream until
They reached the road that led
To Erysichthon's house.
Night had fallen. The great man lay in bed

Snoring too loud to hear his door
Creak open and Hunger slip inside.
Climbing onto the bed, she squatted astride
His chest, then down through his gaping jaw
Inserted her long spoon
And in one deft movement
Emptied him out, then pressed his lips with her own,

Breathing herself into his blood
Till famine blazed there . . . Then out she crept
Back to her hovel. As Erysichthon slept
He started dreaming vividly of food:
Hunks of succulent meat,
In pungent sauces; pies,
Pastries, ripe cheeses; raising a forkful to eat

He ground his teeth on air, and woke
With a strange fierce hunger in his guts . . .
Down at the fridge he rummaged for cold cuts,
Then called his daughter and had her cook
A breakfast of waffles,
Homefries, bacon and eggs,
And wolfed it down. Within an hour or less

He was hungry again, and called
For another breakfast – 'And this time
Don't skimp on me. Let's see, we'll start with a prime
Rib of Black Angus, then a nice grilled
Turkey and Swiss on rye,
Then I think apple cake
With maple whipped cream . . . No, make that pecan
     pie,

Or both in fact.' The girl obeyed.
He gulped down the meal, went off to work
Up at Cascade with his men, where hunger struck
Once again with a pang that made
His flesh pour sweat like wax
From a melting candle:
So about turn, stopping off for Big Macs

And cheese-steaks . . . Back at home he ordered
His dumbstruck daughter to cook him up
'Something substantial. None of this diet crap.
Give me some corned beef hash, some breaded
Pork chops. I want meat loaf,
Donuts and marshmallows,
Bake me some shrimp . . . Don't stand there gaping.
     Move!'

So it continued, day and night;
Daughter cooking while her father ate,
Breaking off only to breathe and defecate
Then only to breathe: his appetite
Was such that he was soon
Obliged to take his meals
(Or rather his one endless meal) on the throne,

Where like an upturned alchemist,
He steadily turned his gold to shit:
Cash, vintage cars, then the yacht, then bit by bit
The land, the house itself, till the last
Dollar slid down the drain
And he and his daughter
Found themselves abruptly out in the rain

Without a penny. What to do?
Beg on street corners? The nickels fell
Like few useless waterdrops in hell
On the flames of his appetite, which grew
Livelier and hotter
Every minute till sheer
Pain brought inspiration: 'I'll sell my daughter!'

So for ten bucks he pimped the child
There on the street (this touching detail
Is taken straight from Ovid's original,
Just in case the reader thinks we've piled
It on a bit too thick);
But while the girl was gone
A sudden pang of hunger like a mule-kick

Stabbed his belly . . . He had to eat
Something, anything, without delay:
Smashing a butcher's window, he grabbed a tray
Of sirloin slabs and fled down the street
Tearing off lumps of steak
With his teeth as he ran
Up out of town to the woods, where like a shark

In a feeding frenzy, he lost
All distinction between what was food
And what was his living flesh: with a jagged

Blade of slate he hacked a plump red roast
From his own arm, the bone
Soon glistened white, stripped bare;
And just as he'd mauled the trees, he mauled his own

Limbs and trunk in a consuming
Fury of hunger and pain until
He'd eaten half his body. A certain pool,
Mentioned before, lay quietly fuming
In the damp air close by:
Here, as Erysichthon
Staggered onward, reeling from tree to tree

Deranged, blood-spattered like a bear
Savaged by wolves – himself both victim
And pack of predators tearing at each limb –
He paused, and lapped the potent water,
Then limped off upward, drawn
By a stumbling instinct
Back to the scene of his desecration.

A sewage ditch now crossed the bulldozed
Building site: he tumbled in, and here
His mutilated shape began to alter
Into its own double-orificed
Essence of greed and waste;
Mouth and rear end opening
To two huge O's; stomach and barrel chest

Hollowing out from rim to rim,
Hardening as his limbs disappeared
And nothing was left of him but a yard
Of concrete pipe. And there we leave him,
Soon to be delivered
From his own emptiness
Forever, or at least until the wood

Reclaims Cascade.
                    Meanwhile beyond,
Much remains still to be spoiled: in Fall
Hillsides still assemble their unsaleable
Red and yellow mosaics; on every pond
Floats the same old mottled
Surrealist carpet; green
Globes of foliage dip themselves in gold

For no discernible purpose.
Then come dustier colours; ochres,
Tawny oranges, browns of bracts and burrs,
Bristly asters, leafless trees like patches
Of worn plush in a once
Sumptuous court's faded
Velvet upholstery, where skeletons

Gemmed with crab-apples breathe a sour
Musk of cider . . . Then winter arrives:
Pathos of moulting angels, arthritic leaves
Gloved by hissing snow that in an hour
Fashions a scrupulous
Translation of each tree
Into a bright new language, and then blows

Its work to pieces, as doubtless
Every translator should. Then springtime's
Mint of glinting coinage – a billion dimes –
Tumbles out of dry twigs; superfluous
Miracle we cherish
Each year more anxiously
As if the very notion of a fresh

Beginning has begun to fray
And seem implausible; as if

Against life's optimistic faith in life
Too much evidence has come to weigh,
And almost everything
It liked about itself
Suddenly seems autumnal, even spring.